MW00952372

Copyright © 2018

This book is a work of nonfiction. Unless otherwise noted the author makes no explicit guarantees as to the accuracy of the information contained in this book.

Unless otherwise indicated, all Scripture quotations are taken from the Holy Bible, New Living Translation, copyright © 1996, 2004, 2015 by Tyndale House Foundation. Used by permission of Tyndale House Publishers, Inc., Carol Stream, Illinois 60188. All rights reserved.

ISBN: 978-1-7315-3095-0

The views expressed in this work are solely those of the author.

Any people depicted in stock imagery provided by Lightstock are models, and such images are being used for illustrative purposes only. Certain stock imagery © Lightstock.

| DEDICATIONS |

To my Lord and Savior who has taught me to not only welcome, but to also embrace the challenges in my life and to see them for what they truly are: a season for growth, an occasion to find rest in your loving arms, and an opportunity to discover that through your strength, guidance and gifts, I'm capable of far more than I ever thought possible.

To my husband, Keith, for being my biggest cheerleader and encourager. I love you and thank God for you every day.

To my boys, Brody and Spencer, who inspire me and help me find the joy in everyday life. I love watching how God is working in your lives and can't wait to see what He has planned for you.

To my friends and family for your unconditional love, support, and prayers through this incredible journey of mine.

| ACKNOWLEDGMENTS |

I'm in awe and so incredibly grateful for how God uses people in our lives, and this devotional would not be possible without the help from many.

Thank you, Keith, Mom, Timberley, and Diona for your endless support, wise counsel, and important input into this book.

Thank you to my friends and family for believing in me. Thank you for your prayers, support, and understanding through my long days in front of the computer and for seeing past the dirty dishes and piles of laundry, so that I could work until the job was done.

Thank you to my launch team for your support, wisdom, and help in getting this devotional into the hands of those who need it most.

Thank you to the FOI community for your encouragement and prayers and for pushing me beyond my comfort zone into creating something that, you too, needed.

| Intro |

I am so excited that you're ready to deepen your relationship with our Almighty Lord. Though I've written this devotional, it is not my journey, it is yours. It is your relationship you are growing with Him.

It is through this journey where you'll learn to find peace in your mess, and that it is possible to experience both pain and joy at the very same time.

I've been where you are, my friend. Down on that valley floor, feeling overwhelmed, extremely frustrated, and ready to give up. I believed that the rest of my life would be filled with pain and that I'd never get out . . . that I'd never find joy this side of heaven. I was believing the lies the enemy was telling me and I know he's feeding them to you as well.

I'm here to tell you, that they are simply not true. I understand the struggle of trying to reflect and focus on God when all you have the energy for is to just get through another day.

It is possible to find joy in the midst of your trials, and that is exactly why I wrote this devotional. To help you see that no matter what your circumstances are, it is not the end of your story, but rather an important road to the incredible life that God created you for.

I understand you are a busy person, so I kept that in mind, making it easy for you to start your day bathed in His Word, even on your most hectic of mornings.

I've also included a "deeper look" section each day so that when you have a bit more time, you'll have a starting point for diving deeper.

The time to begin is right now. So grab your Bible and prayer journal and get to know God better.

I'm praying for you and your journey and can't wait to see the big, beautiful plan that He has for your life.

|DAY 1|

The way to find peace in your mess is by getting to know God and learning to trust in all that He is.

Spend time in The Word getting to know God learning what He has promised you. Psalms 37:4 tells us, "Take delight in the Lord, and He will give you your heart's desires."

He will give you a peace that transcends all understanding. He will help you to succeed and prosper according to His Will.

Talk with God as you go through your day. A quick thank you for the beautiful trees that He's created or the gorgeous, blooming flowers. A thank you for already going before you and equipping you with everything you need to handle the day's challenges.

Begin each prayer by thanking Him rather than immediately jumping in to ask of Him. He wants to fellowship with you throughout the day, not just in the morning and evening.

Today, instead of focusing on your challenges, focus on all the good things that God is. Thank Him throughout this day and trust that He is there to rescue you and help you succeed.

A DEEPER LOOK

Joshua 1:8; Psalm 34:17-19; Philippians 4:6-7; 1 Thessalonians 5:17-18

| Reflections |

Today's Date: _____

_____

_____

_____

_____

_____

_____

_____

_____

_____

_____

_____

_____

_____

_____

| Today's Prayers |

| DAY 2 |

You can find rest in God's loving arms.

Your struggles are tough and difficult to handle, but the victory has already been won. Therefore, go to Him and seek out the rest you so desperately need.

Too many times you try to push through, burning yourself out, insisting on doing it all. Today, God is calling you to rest, to shut down all that is going on around you and seek shelter in Him.

All too often you think that you're the only one who can handle things. But God is so much bigger than you. He already has it all worked out.

He is your rock, He is your salvation. He is where you will find the rest you need to keep going. As it is during this time of rest that He will renew your strength. Find peace in that today.

Today, clear your calendar, turn off your phone, get unplugged and find the rest you so desperately need. Only then will you be able to tackle the challenges that this life throws at you.

A DEEPER LOOK
Matthew 11:28; Psalm 23:1-4; Psalm 62:1

| Reflections |

Today's Date: _____

_____

_____

_____

_____

_____

_____

_____

_____

_____

_____

_____

_____

_____

_____

|Today's Prayers|

| DAY 3 |

You are exactly who God created you to be.

Don't let the enemy convince you otherwise. God made you for a specific purpose, an important job in the body of Christ that only you can fulfill.

Not everyone can go on mission trips across the world. Not everyone can teach or minister.

No matter what season you are in, God will use you for His purpose and only you have the special gifts and talents to fulfill it.

Don't believe the enemy when he tells you that you are not enough. You are bright, beautiful, and the perfect person for God's perfect plan.

With Him, you are stronger and can do far more than you ever dreamed possible. No one else can do what God created you to do. Rejoice in knowing that.

Today, every time the enemy tries to fill you with lies, remember that you are exactly who God created you to be.

A DEEPER LOOK
Jeremiah 29:11; Jeremiah 1:5; 1 Corinthians 12:22; 27

| Reflections |

Today's Date: _____

_____

_____

_____

_____

_____

_____

_____

_____

_____

_____

_____

_____

_____

| Today's Prayers |

|DAY 4|

You have to make the choice to stop worrying.

It's hard not to worry about your everyday circumstances or the emergencies that come your way, but no amount of worry will add a single day to your life. No amount of worry will change the outcome or the circumstances.

The way to fight this is to pray about it. Tell God what you need and thank Him for all He has done.

Every time you start to worry, stop and thank Him for not leaving you and for teaching you in this storm. He knows it takes practice. He knows it's not an easy road, but He never promised it would be.

When you learn to trust in God and let go of the worry, you'll begin to feel that amazing peace that only God can provide. You'll begin to feel joy despite anything you are going through.

Today, make the choice to stop worrying. Put your trust in God, the one who already knows what's going to happen. The One who has promised to bring you through this and to bring glory from it.

A DEEPER LOOK
Philippians 4:6-7; Luke 12:25-26; Matthew 6:31-34

| Reflections |

Today's Date: _____

_____

_____

_____

_____

_____

_____

_____

_____

_____

_____

_____

_____

| Today's Prayers |

| DAY 5 |

God is not mad at you no matter what you've done.

Perhaps you didn't handle a situation as well as you should have. Maybe you said something that you regret. Your God is a patient, merciful, and loving God. He has already forgiven you.

You may have sinned, but you are not that sin. It is no longer your master. You live under the freedom of God's Grace. You were not saved because of the good things you have done, you were saved because He loves you. It is His gift to you.

Because God has already forgiven you, you can forgive yourself. After all, Jesus did not save you so that you could walk around in shame. He saved you so that you can find freedom and peace in this incredible life that He has given you.

Today, remember that there's nothing you've done that God hasn't already forgiven. He delights in showing His unfailing love for you.

A DEEPER LOOK
Daniel 9:9; Romans 6:14; Ephesians 2:8-9; Micah 7:18

| Reflections |

Today's Date: _____

_____

_____

_____

_____

_____

_____

_____

_____

_____

_____

_____

_____

_____

| Today's Prayers |

|DAY 6|

You will have trouble in your life.

The sooner you learn to accept that, the sooner you'll find·peace despite the struggles you go through. It takes a change in perspective, a change in the way you look at the world.

It's not going to be easy and it will require a lot of practice, but it's time to begin thinking of your trials as an opportunity. A chance to learn and grow in your faith. It's when your endurance is strengthened and your character is put to the test.

God will never let harm come to you. He loves you unconditionally and will not let this difficulty destroy you.

Instead, He will use this struggle and bring something beautiful out of it. It may take some time to see, but this is where trusting in God comes in.

Trust in His Strength, His Plan for your life, and His unconditional love for you. He would never let anything destroy someone that He created and loves so much.

Today, thank God for what you are learning and the positive that you know will come out of this struggle. Thank Him for already going before you and equipping you with what you need to handle these challenges, and for the incredible opportunities you know are coming.

A DEEPER LOOK
John 16:33; James 1:2-4; Psalm 138:7;
2 Corinthians 12: 9-10

| Reflections |

Today's Date: _____

_____

_____

_____

_____

_____

_____

_____

_____

_____

_____

_____

_____

_____

_____

| Today's Prayers |

| DAY 7 |

God doesn't expect you to be perfect.

He created you and loves you unconditionally, just as you are. Yes, you should strive to live like Jesus, but you live in a fallen world and you will make mistakes.

Jesus came so that you could be free of not only the big sins, but also the everyday sins like self-pity, envy, and judgment.

When you begin to feel those self-destructive emotions creeping up, remember that God has already forgiven you.

Learn from your mistakes, forgive yourself, move on and do better next time. God is so much bigger than you are, so if He can forgive you, who are you to not forgive yourself? Who are you to not love the person that He created?

Stop dwelling on your shortcomings, things you can't change, and everything you think you aren't. These are all lies from the enemy.

God made you in His perfect image and you have an important job in His kingdom. It's time to stop letting the enemy make you feel less than you are.

You can live in peace today, knowing that you are a member of God's Kingdom. You are wonderfully made in Him.

A DEEPER LOOK
Ecclesiastes 7:20; James 3:2; Colossian 3:15

| Reflections |

Today's Date: _____

_____

_____

_____

_____

_____

_____

_____

_____

_____

_____

_____

_____

_____

_____

| Today's Prayers |

| DAY 8 |

Fear paralyzes, but faith in God empowers.

Fear is one of the enemy's greatest weapons he uses against you.

Don't let him in. Don't let him have that power over you. It's in that deep valley where it is so easy to believe what he's telling you.

When you begin to feel fear, stop and immediately send up a prayer. Remember that God's right beside you, ready to take your hand and walk you through it.

God did not create you to live in constant fear of the next emergency to come your way. When you love your God and know that He is the only one who can get you through this trial, then, and only then, will you be able to drive out the fear in your life.

Today, don't let the enemy get to you. Don't listen to his lies. Instead, fight back with the knowledge that God has you and is stronger than anything the enemy tries to throw at you. Find peace in knowing the true and complete love that God has for you. His love conquers all fear, all trials, and all challenges!

A DEEPER LOOK
2 Timothy 1:7; Psalm 27:1; Psalm 34:4; Psalm 56:3

| Reflections |

Today's Date: _____

_____

_____

_____

_____

_____

_____

_____

_____

_____

_____

_____

_____

_____

_____

_____

| Today's Prayers |

|DAY 9|

God is with you right where you are.

You may be in a dark valley right now, but there's no need to fear. God is with you and has promised to never leave you.

You will not drown in this valley. You will not be destroyed. Yes, it's hard, but you're going to be okay. You will not be here forever, and your life definitely is not over. It is simply a blip in time.

The enemy tells you these lies to keep you down. Don't listen to them. Stand strong in the faith that God is going to pull you through.

He is right beside you in the valley and has promised to never leave you. He is The Light and when it is time, He'll show you the way out.

Gather strength from Him and rejoice in knowing that He is not waiting for your circumstances to improve. Rather He meets you right in the middle of your mess, taking every painstaking step with you! He is ready to provide you with everything you need to get through this.

Turn to Him today and thank Him for walking with you, and for knowing that He is The Light and will guide you every step of the way.

A DEEPER LOOK
Isaiah 43:2; Isaiah 41:10; Joshua 1:9; Psalm 23:4

| Reflections |

Today's Date: _____

| Today's Prayers |

| DAY 10 |

Stop focusing on everything that's wrong in your life and start focusing on everything that's right.

When you're stuck on that valley floor, all too often you start dwelling on everything that' wrong. Yes, you are struggling. Sure, you have a lot going on and when it rains, it downright pours. However, you have far more good things in your life than you do struggles.

Self-pity is not the work of God, it's the work of the enemy and turns your focus to yourself. Jesus did not die for you so that you could walk around feeling sorry for yourself. He was not nailed to the cross so you could wallow in your troubles and unhappiness.

You have a choice to make. You can continue to focus on yourself or you can turn your focus to God and all His glory.

Do you want to continue being miserable? Do you enjoy wallowing in self-pity? Of course, you don't.

Make a list of all the blessings you have in your life. Put them in a notebook, several index cards, or on a list in your phone. Every time you start going down that slippery slope of self-pity and despair, take out your list and read all that you have to be thankful for.

Then go to God and spend the entire prayer thanking Him for all the incredible blessings He has given you. Ask for nothing. If you're short on time, simply whisper "thank you, Jesus," and breathe Him in.

Today, spend your day focusing on all the things that are good in your life and refuse to let the enemy win you over with the self-pity game. Reflect on all that God is and remember that He'll never leave you and will turn this struggle into one of your most treasured blessings.

A DEEPER LOOK
Psalm 73:2-3; Psalm 73: 21-24; Psalm 73:28; James 1:16-17

| Reflections |

Today's Date: _____

| Today's Prayers |

| DAY 11 |

His timing, not yours.

This season is difficult and it's long. It feels like it's never going to end. You're ready to be out of it, certain that you've learned all that you needed to.

But it's not up to you. God's timing is perfect. If you are not yet out of that valley, it's because you still have something to learn. He still has something to teach you.

He has heard your pleas, He has heard your cries and knows you are tired and hurting. He hasn't forgotten you. He is simply preparing the way.

Until then, you are called to be obedient. Open your heart to what He is teaching you and accept that it just takes time.

In the meantime, you can delight in knowing that God is for you. He has a big and beautiful plan like nothing you could have ever envisioned for yourself.

It takes time to prepare the way. It takes time to make sure you're ready for all that He has in store for you.

Today, continue to pray for the desires of your heart, continue seeking His Will for you. Enjoy the green meadows and the beauty in your valley, and be open to what God is teaching you.

It won't be long and God will give you the desires of your heart. It's going to look different than your life right now. Are you ready for it?

Trust in His perfect timing and when it comes, you'll be more than prepared for this new life He is preparing you for.

A DEEPER LOOK
2 Peter 3:9, Acts 1:7; Lamentations 3:25-26; Psalm 27:14

| Reflections |

Today's Date: _____

_____

_____

_____

_____

_____

_____

_____

_____

_____

_____

_____

_____

_____

_____

_____

| Today's Prayers |

| DAY 12 |

Put your trust in God today.

It's time to stop putting your trust in the things of this world. They've let you down time and again.

Learning to put your trust in the Lord takes practice. God knows that, so there's no need to beat yourself up about it. He alone will give you strength. He alone will guide you. You have only to seek Him out.

Today, when you begin to worry, immediately stop yourself and whisper "God, I trust you."

You won't always understand His ways, and that's o.k. You're not meant to. His ways are far better than yours, and you can find great peace in that. How freeing it is that you don't need to have all the answers! You can relax in the knowledge that God's got you.

Turn to Him and ask for guidance. Ask Him to open your eyes and heart to what He is teaching you, to the next step in His plan. You don't need to know how it's all going to play out. All you need is the next step and God will reveal it to you in His perfect timing.

As the One who created you, He knows what you need far better than you do.

Instead of being anxious today, rejoice in the fact that you have one less thing to worry about! Rejoice in knowing that He'll guide you and give you the strength you need to get through this challenge. He's got you. You can trust Him. He's the only One that will never let you down.

A DEEPER LOOK
Psalm 28:7; Proverbs 3:5-6; Isaiah 40:31

| Reflections |

Today's Date: _____

_____
_____
_____
_____
_____
_____
_____
_____
_____
_____
_____
_____
_____
_____

| Today's Prayers |

| DAY 13 |

This valley is merely a blip in time.

This difficulty will pass. The enemy will not win. God has already promised to bring you through it, so there's no need to worry and fret over how and when you're going to get out.

It may be hard and seem like the fight of your life, but it's simply another season. An chance to learn. An opportunity to grow closer to God and learn how to put your complete trust in Him.

With God by your side, this fight has already been won. You may say "I can not do this," but with God, you can know without a shadow of a doubt that "together, we can."

Stay obedient. Keep turning to Him. Don't let the enemy fill your head with lies like, "this is the end," "this is what your life is going to look like from here on out," because they simply aren't true.

Today, remember to be patient. This season is simply that . . .a season in your life that will pass. Stay strong and obedient, intentionally choose joy each and every day. Choose to trust in knowing that God will provide for you and He will reward you because of the way you handled this season.

A DEEPER LOOK
Romans 12:12; Galatians 6:9; James 5:8; Lamentations 3:25-26

| Reflections |

Today's Date: _____

| Today's Prayers |

| DAY 14 |

Let His Peace wash over you.

Today, work on not being anxious. Every time you begin to feel that tickle of the enemy trying to make you feel scared and upset, stop, whisper God's name, and breathe Him in.

God didn't create you to be unhappy and live a life of worry and fear. He wants you to feel His peace. He wants you to experience joy.

Jesus saved you so that you could experience this wonderful life on earth, free from the chains of fear and apprehension you're living all the time.

He already fought the hardest battle for you, so there's nothing left to be anxious about. Anything life throws at you is a walk in the park compared to what Jesus went through.

Find joy in Him. Make a choice to enjoy all that He has created for you and all that He created you for.

Today, choose joy.

A DEEPER LOOK
Philippians 4:6-7; Psalm 94:19; 1 Thessalonians 5:16

| Reflections |

Today's Date: _____

| Today's Prayers |

| DAY 15 |

God rescues the brokenhearted.

God is never far from the brokenhearted. He rescues those who are suffering and bandages their wounds.

This battle you are in is hard. It's exhausting and, at times, you may be ready to quit, wanting to just pull the covers over your head and not get out of bed.

It's in those times God is calling you to rest. He knows you are broken. He knows you lack the strength and energy to keep going.

It's okay to rest. In fact, it's necessary to recharge in order to be ready for all that the enemy tries to throw at you.

Turn to God who is right beside you, holding you by your right hand. He's ready to soothe your pain and offer you comfort. He's ready to give you rest and strengthen you for the remainder of your fight. You have only to turn to Him.

You must go through this valley in order to see the glory waiting for you on the other side. It's imperative in order to grow.

Today, accept that you need rest. Open your heart to the fact that God is your source of joy and will deliver it to you on that valley floor. All you have to do is receive it.

Accept the comfort and peace that He is offering you in this period of necessary rest.

A DEEPER LOOK
Psalm 147:3; Psalm 34:17-19; Nehemiah 8:10

| Reflections |

Today's Date: _____

_____

_____

_____

_____

_____

_____

_____

_____

_____

_____

_____

_____

_____

_____

| Today's Prayers |

| DAY 16 |

Go to God confidently in your prayers.

God promises that when you trust in Him and His plan for you, you can go to Him with confidence.

Do not waver and He will give you your heart's desire. Do not be timid, go before Him boldly. Trust in Him. Be confident in all that He is and all that He will do for you.

When trials arise, and you already have a relationship with God, there'll be no reason to waver. No need to waste time being timid in what you need from Him. All you have to do is confidently ask and you'll already know that He will show up.

He will provide the grace, strength, and guidance you need to see you through this challenge.

Part of learning to trust in Him means going through the hard times. It's in these seasons that He teaches you to trust in Him. It's where He'll show you that His Strength is made stronger in your weakness.

He doesn't like to see you hurt, but He will allow these challenges so that you learn to grow and put your complete trust in Him and His mighty works.

A DEEPER LOOK
1 John 5:14-15; Ephesians 3:12; Hebrews 4:16

|Reflections|

Today's Date: _____

_____

_____

_____

_____

_____

_____

_____

_____

_____

_____

_____

_____

_____

_____

_____

_____

| Today's Prayers |

| DAY 17 |

You're not always going to understand the struggles in your life.

It's not always for you to understand why you're going through this struggle. You are called to be obedient and press on.

This struggle may be bigger than you can comprehend. It's okay. God isn't calling you to understand it, He's calling you to be obedient through it all.

The enemy is telling you that it's not meant for good, that you don't deserve to go through this, and the struggle has lasted long enough. Don't believe his lies. Don't let him steal your joy. He doesn't want what's best for you. He doesn't love you unconditionally. God does and He has a big and beautiful plan in all of this. He's going to work it all out for your good!

Seek God's counsel in all that you do. Ask him to guide you. Understand that you don't need to know the big picture. In fact, find freedom in that! You no longer have to worry over how it's all going to play out. Instead, simply ask God to show you the next step in His plan and then find peace in knowing that He has it all under control and will work it out in His perfect timing.

A DEEPER LOOK
John 10:10; Romans 8:28; Proverbs 3:5-6

| Reflections |

Today's Date: _____

| Today's Prayers |

| DAY 18 |

Life is glorious and meant to be lived that way.

Life is hard, no doubt about it, but it's certainly not bad. There is incredible beauty found in knowing that life is good.

Don't believe the lies the enemy is telling you, making you believe something that is simply not true.

When he tries to get in your head, don't let him. Turn to God, breathe Him in. He will crush the enemy and open your eyes to the magnificent beauty that even this valley has to offer you.

Believe what God is telling you. Remember that He is good, He loves you unconditionally, and that anything that happens to you in this lifetime is no match for Him.

Find joy in knowing that no matter how deep your valley is, there are still green meadows and peaceful streams and God will walk with you every step of the way. He will provide the necessary rest, shelter and protection you need.

Today, open your eyes. Look for the green meadows and peaceful streams that are found on that valley floor and enjoy the breathtaking beauty of it all.

A DEEPER LOOK
2 Samuel 22:30; Philippians 4:8; Psalm 23:1-4

|Reflections|

Today's Date: _____

_____

_____

_____

_____

_____

_____

_____

_____

_____

_____

_____

_____

_____

| Today's Prayers |

| DAY 19 |

Let your faith be bigger than your fear.

You are not going through this life alone. You have The One who created you, who knows you inside and out right beside you. He is the light shining your way.

Put your faith in God and all that He is and you'll start to see your fears disappear.

God promises that He will never leave you. He promises that He, alone, can take away your worries and save you. When your faith in God is bigger than your fear, the enemy has absolutely no power over you.

There's nothing the enemy can throw at you that God can not defeat. You can find comfort in knowing that God goes before you, taking care of most of what the enemy tries to defeat you with. And what does make it to you, God equips you with everything you need to handle that challenge. He uses that obstacle to teach you, to make you stronger, and to build your character.

The best way to handle the challenges that come at you every day is to start your day knowing and learning the truth. The truth that even with faith as small as a mustard seed, you can still move mountains.

Throughout the day, reach out to God, whisper His name and let His Peace wash over you.

Today, let your faith be bigger than your fear. And then prepare yourself, because you're about to move mountains!

A DEEPER LOOK
Isaiah 35:4; Psalm 118:6; Deuteronomy 31:6; Matthew 17:20

| Reflections |

Today's Date: _____

| Today's Prayers |

| DAY 20 |

Stop hiding behind your scars.

You've got nothing to be ashamed of. This trial you are going through is hard, but you're learning.

Learning to put your complete trust in Him, learning that no matter how difficult life gets, it's not going to destroy you and that you can still find joy no matter what the enemy throws at you.

You are growing stronger, happier, and opening yourself up to the many opportunities this challenge is bringing you. Opportunities that can only be achieved by going through the valley.

Don't hide behind your scars in shame. Instead, celebrate them, for a scar is merely proof that you are surviving, that you are succeeding, and most importantly, they are proof that God heals.

So today, don't hide behind the shame of the valley you are in. Rather stand tall, rejoice that your God loves you unconditionally and that He will never leave you. Rejoice in knowing something big and beautiful is coming your way, and that you're making it through. You're learning to find peace despite anything that happens to you.

A DEEPER LOOK
1 Peter 4:16; Psalm 29:11; 1 Corinthians 10:13

| Reflections |

Today's Date: _____

| Today's Prayers |

| DAY 21 |

God will give you the strength to get through this.

You may be sick and tired of being sick and tired. You may be growing weary in this fight, but God's got you. His strength is sufficient for you. You don't have to be strong enough on your own.

God will provide all that you need and give you the endurance to keep fighting. He will guide you when you don't know which step to take next.

There is no doubt that this is a difficult journey, but you can't let the enemy fool you into believing that there's no way out. It's just another lie he's telling you. Don't listen to him.

Fight him by turning to God, your one and only source of strength. He's waiting right beside you. All you have to do is ask him for guidance. Ask for strength and endurance to get you through.

When Jesus was heading to the cross, He knew that He could endure the pain because of what was on the other side. You, too, can endure your pain because you know that you're growing. You know that God has a big, beautiful plan waiting for you on the other side of this valley.

Know that you aren't on this journey alone. You don't need to have the strength to fight the enemy, God is right beside you and provides all the strength you need.

Today, find peace in that.

A DEEPER LOOK
Isaiah 40:29; 31; Hebrews 12:1-2; Philippians 4:13

| Reflections |

Today's Date: _____

| Today's Prayers |

| DAY 22 |

Seek refuge in God, not in people or possessions in this life.

So many of your struggles come from having high expectations of earthly things and people. Anything that is of this earth is not guaranteed. Only God will be there for you 100% of the time, day or night.

God created you, therefore, He knows exactly what you need. He knows the strengths, gifts, and talents that He created in you and knows how best to use them to help you succeed, to help you get through this trial.

Possessions of this earth will only bring you temporary joy. Money, success, power, and acquiring "more things," are not the answer to this valley you are in. They may feel good for a moment, but they won't provide the everlasting peace you are searching for.

People are of this earth and are flawed, not capable of bringing the true peace and companionship that only Jesus can provide for you. God may use them to help you through this, but they, alone, can not give you the strength to get you through. When God puts them in your path, listen and let them help guide you, but don't put them before God.

Have faith in Him. Draw upon His Strength every single day. Whisper to Him throughout the day. Even whispering a simple, "Jesus," will give you unimaginable strength.

Today, stop looking to things of this earth to bring you the peace and joy you so desperately crave, so desperately need. Instead, turn to Him for the only kind of peace and joy that will last and never let you down.

A DEEPER LOOK
Psalm 118:8; Ecclesiastes 5:10; 1 John 2:15-17; Matthew 6:19-21

|Reflections|

Today's Date: _____

| Today's Prayers |

| DAY 23 |

God knows your struggle is hard.

Grant yourself some grace, learn from it and move on.

If God understands this, then you need to extend yourself some grace as well.

Grace to rest when you need it. Grace to learn to manage this struggle. Grace from the guilt you so often feel for not always handling everything exactly the way you should.

Today, accept that grace. Learn from what you've been through so far, make a change in how you're handling it, both mentally and logistically, and move on.

Remember, this is an opportunity to learn. When you can recognize that, you'll get through this struggle a lot faster. You'll come out of it a lot stronger.

Reflect on the struggle you are in right now. How have you handled it? Not as good as you'd like? It's okay. Learn from it. Ask God to guide you in your journey and take the next step. It's time for you to stop looking backward.

You've got this. You're growing from this. Rejoice and choose to find joy in that today.

A DEEPER LOOK
Philippians 3:13-14; James 1:2-4; Galatians 6:9

| Reflections |

Today's Date: _____

| Today's Prayers |

| DAY 24 |

The enemy may be strong,
but the Spirit of Christ is stronger.

You can find peace in knowing that God is stronger than anything the enemy tries to throw at you. No matter how deep your valley is right now, God has you. He's got the strength and power to give you rest and bring you out of it.

The enemy is not fighting you because you're weak. He's fighting you because you have the power of God within you. Determine today to stop letting the enemy get ahold of you. Stop believing the lies he keeps telling you.

You are strong. You are loved. God has a plan for you and the way to that plan is through this valley you are in. So stop letting the enemy tell you that God doesn't love you, that life is too hard and will always be this way.

Turn to God and ask Him for the strength, endurance, and guidance to get through. Know that He will not lead you into anything that will cause you harm. It may not be easy, but it's the hardest trials that reap the best rewards.

Rejoice in knowing that God's plan for you requires this path and that it won't break you, but rather will bring you victory. It will bring you a life that shows you that you are far more capable than you thought.

If God has the power to raise Jesus from the dead, then He certainly has the power to defeat the enemy and help you through this trial.

So today, turn to God. Ask Him for His strength and endurance. Don't listen to the enemy when he tries to fill your head with lies. Know that he can't get through to you because you have the power of Christ within you.

A DEEPER LOOK
Psalm 73:26; Psalm 34:17; Romans 8:11

| Reflections |

Today's Date: _____

_____

_____

_____

_____

_____

_____

_____

_____

_____

_____

_____

_____

_____

_____

| Today's Prayers |

| DAY 25 |

It's impossible to be stressed
when you're focused on how blessed you are.

When you're staring down the face of, yet, another trial in your life, it's hard to remember all the incredible blessings you've been given. But you have a choice. . . to stay in the stress of this trial you're in, or find joy and focus on all the blessings that you've been given.

Today, make that choice to reflect on all the blessings you have. Go to God and thank Him for the wonderful gifts He's given you.

Think back and consider the fact that He has given you absolutely everything you've ever needed. It may not have been everything you wanted, but if He didn't provide those things, then they weren't good for you anyway. So you can find peace in that.

Take note of all the blessings you've been given in this world and start your prayers by thanking Him. Thank Him for providing for all your needs, the beautiful scenery you see driving to work or carpool, for the money that He provides for you, because, in His mighty way, it is always enough to sustain you.

Thank Him for the guidance He's giving you. Even in the midst of a difficult challenge, you can still thank Him because you know that he is teaching you something big and that He will bring something beautiful out of these ashes. Thank Him for already knowing He's taking care of you.

Today, stop focusing on how stressed you are and instead, focus on the glorious blessings you've been given.

A DEEPER LOOK
1 Thessalonians 5:18; James 1:17;
1 Chronicles 16:34; Philippians 4:6

| Reflections |

Today's Date: _____

| Today's Prayers |

|DAY 26|

Don't panic when trials and challenges come your way.

You already know difficulties are coming. It's certainly no surprise! In fact, scripture tells you, here on earth you will have many trials and sorrows. But knowing that He has already overcome the world, that He has already won the battle can bring you comfort today.

You don't have to be strong enough, and in fact, you aren't strong enough to get through these trials. But God is and He will take you by your right hand and bring you through this.

Continual prayer and spending time in The Word will give you the confidence you need when emergencies come your way.

When they do, take a deep breath, confidently go to God and ask for guidance, strength, and endurance. And then wait patiently, as He's about to show you the glory that can come from this struggle and it's going to be beautiful.

A DEEPER LOOK
John 16:33; Deuteronomy 31:6;
Isaiah 41:13; Hebrews 4:16

| Reflections |

Today's Date: _____

| Today's Prayers |

| DAY 27 |

For when you are weak, then you are strong.

God is going to use your weakness, trials, and difficulties for something bigger than you could ever imagine.

You may be fighting right now. You may be weary and exhausted. You may feel like giving up, but you can find peace in this challenge because His power works best in your weakness. Only God can take such a difficult season and bring beauty out of the ashes, and what feels like complete ruin.

God is your salvation in times of trouble. He is your source of strength, your protector and your rock.

You are not alone. God's intention was never to have you go through life on your own. He longs to have you turn to Him all day every day for help. He wants to give you guidance in the next step in your journey, rest when you need it, and the strength and power to not just get through this valley, but to find the beauty in it. To get to the other side victoriously, stronger and more importantly, closer to Him.

He's waiting right beside you. Ready to help. Today, all you have to do is turn to Him and ask.

A DEEPER LOOK
2 Corinthians 12:9-10; Isaiah 40:29, 31; Philippians 4:13; Isaiah 33:2

| Reflections |

Today's Date: _____

_____

_____

_____

_____

_____

_____

_____

_____

_____

_____

_____

_____

_____

_____

| Today's Prayers |

| DAY 28 |

God uses ordinary people to do extraordinary things.

This struggle you are in is not too difficult or sinful for God.

He has the power to use it for good. He has the power to bring you out the other side victoriously. When He does, it will not only show you that you are capable of so much more, it will also show others His full glory.

You may wonder how God could use a person like yourself. Someone who is a broken and weary sinner. But you mustn't forget that God uses ordinary people to do His work. People who are not afraid to say yes.

If God can use a murderer to spread the gospel, he can use you. If God can use an ordinary, young woman to become Jesus' earthly mother, He can use you. If God can use a young boy to defeat Goliath, he can use you. If God can use a man to lead his people out of the land of his adopted family, He, most certainly, can use you.

When you learn to find peace on that valley floor, when you learn that true joy can be found only in God and not in things of this earth, God will use you to be a blessing to others. He wants you to share your journey and help others through their trials. You have been blessed to be a blessing.

There's only one person who can claim to be perfect. For the rest, you get through these struggles and difficulties with God and the people that He places in your life. Perhaps, he's calling you to do this for someone else today.

You may not be ready yet, and that's okay. God knows the perfect time, but when He calls, will you be willing to say yes?

A DEEPER LOOK
Exodus 9:16, Acts 4:13, 1 Timothy 1:15-16, 2 Timothy 1:9

| Reflections |

Today's Date: _____

_____

_____

_____

_____

_____

_____

_____

_____

_____

_____

_____

_____

_____

_____

_____

_____

| Today's Prayers |

| DAY 29 |

You no longer need to fear life's trials.

Obstacles are going to be thrown at you throughout your entire life. You already know this.

They are hard, they are complicated, and sometimes they take the wind right out of you, but you no longer need to fear them.

They may knock you down a time or two, but they can't defeat you.

You're persevering. You're growing stronger and learning that you're far more capable than you ever thought you could be. You're building character.

With God by your side, you're able to endure the storms and withstand anything that life throws at you. You're learning that you can trust God in every situation in your life, and in fact, you need Him more than you need air to breathe. He is the one and only sustainer of life. Your creator will never let anything destroy you or put you through anything that you can't handle without Him.

That is something to celebrate, something to find comfort in. You are growing. You are maturing, and you're learning to find peace right in the middle of your mess.

Today, celebrate the obstacles that keep coming your way. Because of them, you are growing stronger!

A DEEPER LOOK
Romans 5:3-5; Isaiah 41:10; Psalm 46:1

| Reflections |

Today's Date: _____

_____

_____

_____

_____

_____

_____

_____

_____

_____

_____

_____

_____

_____

_____

| Today's Prayers |

| Day 30 |

You are blessed to be a blessing.

Maybe you're still in the valley. Perhaps God is bringing you out of it. Maybe you are out and victoriously on the other side. No matter where you are in this season, you've been blessed.

God did not bring you through it to keep it to yourself. He brought you through it to be a blessing to others.

It may not be on a big scale, it may even be right in your own backyard, but wherever He is leading you, whoever He puts in your path, it's for a reason.

Be open to the fact that He may be calling you to help someone else through their difficult journey.

If so, be a person that does not hide in shame, but rather show others that we're all in or have been on that valley floor, and there is absolutely nothing to be ashamed of.

There is something beautiful that can be found in those trials. Show them that God, in all His glory, will get them through it. Point them to Him and all that He can do for them.

Accept it. In fact, embrace it and let God use you to be a blessing to someone else.

A DEEPER LOOK
1 Thessalonians 5:11; Matthew 5:16; Genesis 12:2

| Reflections |

Today's Date: _____

| Today's Prayers |

| FINAL THOUGHTS |

This is not the end of your journey. In fact, it's only the beginning. The beginning of a steadfast, peace-filled life. A life where you can celebrate His unconditional love for you and know that He alone, is the source of your peace.

Remember that when you trust in God completely, you always have His Truth to stand on, His Light to guide your way.

When life tries to throw you off track again, go to God immediately and thank Him because of who you are and, more importantly, who He is.

You now know that you are not alone and that He has promised to never leave you. You'll consider it an opportunity. . . to grow, to learn, to fight like crazy with God leading the way. It'll be another chance to spend more time with Him, to trust in that which you cannot see!

Don't forget to open your eyes on that valley floor! You won't want to miss those beautiful green meadows and peaceful, meandering streams down there. The perfect place to find rest in the middle of your storm.

Until next time...

Made in the USA
Lexington, KY
03 March 2019